TACKLE
BOXING

Henry Cooper
with Norman Giller

Stanley Paul
London Melbourne Auckland Johannesburg

Stanley Paul & Co. Ltd

An imprint of Century Hutchinson Ltd

62–65 Chandos Place, London WC2N 4NW

Century Hutchinson (Australia) Pty Ltd
16–22 Church Street, Hawthorn, Melbourne, Victoria 3122

Century Hutchinson (NZ) Ltd
PO Box 40–086, Glenfield, Auckland 10

Century Hutchinson (SA) Pty Ltd
PO Box 337, Bergvlei 2012, South Africa

First published 1988
© Henry Cooper and Norman Giller 1988

Set in Plantin $10\frac{1}{2}/12$ pt

Printed and bound in Great Britain by
Butler and Tanner Ltd, Frome, Somerset

British Library Cataloguing in Publication Data
Cooper, Henry, *1934*–
    Tackle boxing.
    1. Boxing
    I. Title   II. Giller, Norman
    796.8'3   GV1133

ISBN 0 09 166081 5

TACKLE BOXING

Contents

Acknowledgements

The authors and publishers would like to thank Associated Press, Sport & General Press Agency and Press Association for permission to reproduce their copyright photographs, and David Woodroffe for his illustrations; also ITV's 'Voice of Boxing' Reg Gutteridge for his constructive input.

Introduction

Beauty, so they say, is in the eye of the beholder, and boxing is for me a beautiful sport if performed with proper skill and technique. The objective of this book is to help you learn to box the champions' way and I hope that, whether you are a beginner or an accomplished boxer looking for some refresher tips, you will find inspiration and incentive on the following pages.

I have called on my 25 years of ring experience as an amateur and professional boxer to give hard-earned advice on how you can develop and improve your ability, and wherever possible I have given examples of how great champions have executed the punches and moves that are described in detail. Where this book differs from other instruction manuals that I have read is that we have not gone in for the stilted posed pictures of unknown boxers showing how it should be done. My co-author Norman Giller and I have been through dozens of photographic files to find action shots of outstanding champions displaying the skills that can help make you a more efficient and understanding boxer.

Boxing has always been good to me and now I want to try to give something back by passing on what I have learned about a great character-building sport that is not only a matter of skill but also of courage, self-discipline, dedication and physical excellence. During my happy association with the televised amateur boxing tournament on Channel 4, I have been asked repeatedly to recommend a book that helps to teach boys to box 'like the champions do'. So we have produced this book to try to meet the demand.

I hope this book helps *you* box the champions' way.

1
The Punches

The Jab

This is the bread-and-butter punch that every boxer needs to develop. Without it you are likely to remain a hungry fighter! I rate it the most important of all the punches because it lays the foundation for everything that follows. If you've got a solid jab to the head in your armoury it means you can compile points from a distance, keep your opponent off balance and create openings for your right hand (or left if you are a southpaw).

For greatest effect the jab should be thrown with speed and strength in line from the shoulder and in twos or threes. A helpful little reminder you can give yourself is: 'Don't forget the postman's knock.' This will underline the fact that you need to make a rat-a-tat delivery of the jab. You will often hear a second calling from a corner: 'Double them up.' It's an instruction to throw jabs in quick succession. If you are in distance with the first jab it's odds on that the following jab – released instantly – will land on the same target area.

You can make the most of your reach by standing side on and leading with the left (or right, if you're a southpaw). It means you are presenting the narrowest target for your opponent who needs to get past your lead before he can land with effective punches of his own. If your jab is constantly in his face it stops him from composing himself for an attack and if you are standing side on it makes it really difficult for him to get into range with his punches. Joe Louis, Muhammad Ali, Larry Holmes, Sonny Liston and Ernie Terrell are heavyweight champions who spring to mind as having possessed textbook left jabs. It would be well worth your while studying their technique on video if you get the chance.

The execution: To give your jab extra authority it should be delivered with shoulder strength behind it. Too many jabs that I see are just 'arm' blows that carry little weight and can be easily brushed aside. The punch must flow smoothly with a final snapping action and just before the moment of impact there

---

The short left jab. *Tony Sibson did not enjoy many moments of mastery against Marvin Hagler in their 1983 world middleweight title fight in New York, but here he is landing a short left jab. The left jab is seldom, if ever, a knockout blow; but many bouts are won by the skilful use of it. It can be used to keep your opponent off balance and thus create openings for other more powerful blows*

should be a slight turn of the hip and shoulder that will give the blow that vital jolting power. Slide your leading left foot (or right if you're a southpaw) half a pace forward just a split second before landing so that your weight balance is momentarily on the front foot. The heel of your back foot should be an inch or two off the canvas with the weight on the toes. For the best results the jab should come straight from the shoulder and then return on that same path. Your arm can be relaxed in the early stages of the delivery but then straighten it out in that final moment before impact.

Turn your wrist in the last couple of inches so that as the knuckle part of your fist makes contact with your opponent's head the palm is facing the canvas. It's important to remember to keep your non-punching hand guarding your face and your elbow tucked comfortably into your waistline to ward off punches to the head and body. The movement you are making in throwing the jab means that your jaw is automatically being protected by the leading shoulder.

Pro-tip: Get a sparring partner or trainer to put on large coaching pad-gloves so that you can practise throwing your jabs against a moving target. Start off by throwing just one jab at intervals until you are happy with the 'feel' of both the punch and your weight balance. When you feel comfortable bring the postman's knock into operation, sending out rat-a-tat jabs in rapid succession. Don't worry too much in the early stages about your weight distribution. If you are delivering the punch correctly you will find this comes automatically. Ask somebody, preferably a trainer with some ring knowledge, to stand to one side watching you and he should be able to gauge whether you have the weight correctly balanced at the moment of launching and landing.

Alternative Jabs

The straight-from-the-shoulder jab should be the first punch that you master. But there are alternative ways to use the jab to good effect and to stop yourself becoming predictable. After convincing your opponent that you are a conventional straight left (or right) lead man, you can surprise him by firing a jab

The jab from a crouch. *Randolph Turpin (right) was arguably the greatest of all Britain's post-war champions. He was a dynamic puncher but it was his straight left work that won him the world middleweight crown from the legendary Sugar Ray Robinson in London in July 1952. Here we see Randy surprising Sugar Ray with a classic left jab from a crouching position. He has slipped Robinson's lead and has driven the jab strong and true to the chin. Notice the way Randy has got his right fist ready to throw for a one-two connection*

from waist level on an upwards trajectory and straight through the middle of his guard.

The rules of delivery are similar to those for the straight jab but the power comes more from the turn of the hips than the shoulder. Then there is the jab to the body, released from a crouching position and often immediately followed by a jab to the head. The jab to the body can have the effect of bringing your opponent's guard down but as you have gone into a crouch be prepared to avoid counter-punches because you are in a more vulnerable position than when standing upright. Bob Fitzsimmons, British-born former world middle, light-heavy and heavyweight champion, threw the most famous of all straight lefts to the body. He knocked out 'Gentleman' Jim Corbett with the punch to win the world heavyweight crown in 1897. It landed in the pit of Corbett's stomach and became known as the solar plexus punch.

The only occasions when I feel that it is justified to throw an 'arm' lead – that is without weight behind it – is when you are using it as a feint or a range-finder, tapping out a couple of leads before following up with a sudden full-weight punch that could take your opponent by surprise.

A lot of capital can be gained from using the left jab as a counter-punch after blocking or slipping your opponent's lead and I cover this useful punch in the section on countering.

I cannot emphasize strongly enough the importance of practising and perfecting the straight left (or straight right if you're a southpaw). Keep stabbing the lead out in front of a full-length mirror and while shadow boxing; work with it also on the punchbag and, best of all, during sparring sessions until you have it mastered so that you can deliver the jab with power, confidence and accuracy. It may never be your most spectacular punch but it's the weapon that can build vital points and prove a continual source of irritation to your opponents.

The Hook

The left hook was my most explosive punch and I admit to some bias when I say that if delivered with perfect timing and pinpoint accuracy it is the finest punch in boxing. Most boxing coaches preach that it is primarily a counter-punch but I found it could also be a lethal attacking weapon. The tips I give for using the left hook can be translated by southpaws for their right hook. All the basic rules are the same.

The hook is a bent-arm punch and can be thrown to head or body with equal effect. Kid McCoy, world welterweight champion just before the turn of the century, is credited with having been the first fighter to introduce the punch. He

Turning the hips. *Smokin' Joe Frazier lands the punch that clinched victory in the 'Fight of the Century' against Muhammad Ali in New York in March 1971. This mighty left hook floored Ali in the 15th and final round. The punch has come with a swivel of the hips and it has been delivered with shoulder strength. And, as with all the best punches, there is a natural follow-through. I honestly don't know how Ali managed to get himself up off the canvas after taking this almighty thump on the jaw. There had been little to choose between them, but the knockdown swayed the judges towards Frazier and he was awarded a points decision*

developed it after being told how the bore in a rifle spun a bullet, sending it faster, truer and with devastating results. He landed the punch with an exaggerated twist of the wrist and it became known as the Corkscrew Punch. The screwing of the wrist gives that extra snap on impact.

An important point when preparing to throw the hook is that you shouldn't advertise it by suddenly moving to a square-on stance. I often see even seasoned professionals make this cardinal error, yet they might just as well send their opponent a postcard to say the left hook is on its way. Practise delivering it from a side-on stance, pivoting at the hips and shoulder and transferring the weight to the right foot with the leading leg turning inwards on the ball of the foot. Keep throwing it until it becomes a smooth, spontaneous movement. The hook is not a punch you should think about. It's got to come naturally.

It can be a risky punch to fire because you are briefly having to leave the left side of your face unguarded, but if you have perfected it your opponent is going to be too busy trying to take evasive action to attempt unloading a punch of his own. It need not be a long punch. Joe Louis was one of the greatest hookers of all time and he sometimes knocked out opponents with a paralysing left hook that travelled no more than eight or nine inches.

It is worth mentioning here that long punches may look spectacular but they are often not nearly as effective as those that take the shortest route to the target and they also eat up a lot more energy. When you see big swinging punches they have usually run out of full power by the time they have landed and the opponent is given time in which to take defensive action.

The execution: The left hook is thrown with a whiplash action and with a powerful twist of the body from the hips. Just before release the arm should be relaxed and bent at the elbow. Don't tense up before letting the punch go because you will find this will spoil your timing and the final effect. I know that when, for instance, I dropped Cassius Clay (as he was then) in our 1963 fight at Wembley I did not feel a thing as I landed my left hook on his chin. It was a relaxed punch that travelled in an arc over his lowered right arm and I automatically followed through with the punch after making contact.

It is vital with all punches, particularly the hook, to hit *through* rather than *at* the target. A split second before impact turn the wrist so that the knuckle part of your glove almost screws into the target area with your palm pointing inward. You have to summon all your strength into that last moment before impact but you must do it without tensing. From the moment of launching the punch your hooked arm should be swept towards the target with speed but don't plant power into the fist until literally inches from the impact point.

Pro-tip: One of the most effective uses of the left hook is when it is thrown off the jab. Practise throwing a straight left lead and then immediately following with a hook. The objective is to throw a fast jab to the head and then all in the same movement take a quick step forward with the left foot, turning the shoulder and hip and firing a hook. If it is done quickly and efficiently enough, your opponent will instinctively be preparing his defence for a following left jab and will be unable to block a hook suddenly coming in at an angle out of his line of vision. There were many times during my 25-year career as an amateur and professional when my opponents would say after I had either knocked them out or off their feet: 'I didn't see what hit me.' That was because I was bringing the old hook round out of their view. I was getting in through the side door while they had their eyes fixed on the front. Hooking off the jab is one of the most lethal combinations of all and it is well worth spending hours getting it smoothed out in training, practising on the punchbag and with sparring partners. I promise that all the work you do in the gym will be well rewarded in the ring when you have the satisfaction of landing this sweetest of double blows.

The perfect punch. *This is the most striking picture I have seen of one of the best – and certainly most publicised – left hooks I ever threw. It caught Muhammad Ali (or Cassius Clay as he was then) flush on the right side of the jaw at Wembley Stadium in June 1963. The picture usually published of the punch shows Clay dropping back into the ropes, but the beauty of this photograph for instructive purposes is that it gives the ideal example of how you must follow through. I cannot stress enough times how important it is to hit* through *rather than* at *the target. A split second before impact turn the wrist so that the knuckle part of your glove almost screws into the target with your palm pointing inward. My weight balance here has shifted from my left side to my right to get the maximum body power behind the punch. This was the first time Clay had been knocked down in his career and – excuse me for blowing my own trumpet – this picture captures the perfect execution of a left hook. That's the good news. The bad news for me was that Clay got up as the bell rang to end the fourth round. He stopped me with a cut eye in the fifth round*

The Body Hook

This is a specialist punch that takes hours of practice to sharpen but if you can get it right it will become among your most potent weapons. One of the best exponents I've ever seen of the left hook to the body is Irish idol Barry McGuigan. He has always given the impression that the punch comes naturally to him but he admits he has spent years getting it right.

Barry went to extremes to master the punch, tying his right hand with string so that it was immobile and then throwing hundreds of left hooks to the body until he was letting it go without thinking. Once he had got the delivery exactly right he then started to concentrate on the landing area, ensuring that he could get the best possible results from the punch.

After advice from top American trainer Bobby McQuillar, he decided to aim as often as possible for the liver region of the upper abdomen, an area that cannot be built up with protective muscle. I used to favour going for the solar plexus at the pit of the stomach, but you need deadly accuracy because just an inch or two lower and you would be risking disqualification for hitting low.

The execution: The left hook to the body is swept up from below the hip in a half-hook, half-uppercut movement. You need your weight slightly on your left side and your knees should be bent at the start of a punch that needs to be delivered from close range for full effect. It has to be fired in one smooth motion, pivoting your hips and shoulders and with all the weight of your body swung forward onto your right foot. Turn your wrist just before making contact so that the palm of your hand is facing up. You can knock the wind out of an opponent with this punch, or at the very least force him to drop his guard and give you an opportunity for an attack to the head.

Pro-tip: When practising the hook to the body make sure your chin is tucked down. You need to drop your shoulder and arm ready for launching the punch and so for a fleeting moment there is an inviting opening for an opponent with a fast right hand. Don't make it an even more inviting target by hanging your chin out as if to dry. Once you are happy with the timing of your hooks to the head and body, start doubling them up, hooking to the body and then to the head in a quick flowing movement. Get it right on the punchbag and then try it out in sparring. I warn you that it's not easy to master but perseverance will pay off. If you can support a solid jab with heavy hooks to the head and body you are well on your way to becoming a formidable boxer.

The Right Cross

The right cross usually follows a left lead or a feinted left in a rhythmic one-two movement. It is similar in style of delivery to a left hook and can be devastating if your timing is spot-on and you follow through with the punch from the shoulder. You get the greatest results from the right cross when your opponent is moving to his left and so into the path of the punch, and if you can get his attention drawn to your left hand all the better.

The right cross. *Mike Tyson delivers a powerful right cross against Trevor Berbick in the second round of their heavyweight title fight in Las Vegas in November 1986. 'Iron Mike' became the youngest world heavyweight champion shortly after when the referee intervened. Note how he has punched* through *the target*

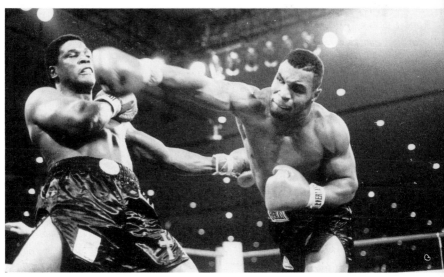

The execution: The right cross is delivered from the classic, upright stance with the right hand held high at a starting-point alongside your cheekbone. It is rarely used as a lead punch, but rather as a follow-up to a left lead. You must throw it quickly and with a swift shift of weight from the right foot to the left as you make the connection, preferably against the jaw or the left side of the head.

Follow-through is all-important, and the swivel of your hips and right shoulder will give you the impetus that adds jolting power to the punch. If you are delivering it correctly the punch should drive over the top of your opponent's left hand and into

---

Ideal Holmes. *Larry Holmes had a wide variety of combination punches which helped him win 48 successive fights. Here we see him finishing off a one–two against Gerry Cooney, following a left jab with a crashing right cross. He has cleverly evaded the jab from Cooney and has still managed to stay in punching range. Holmes retained his world heavyweight crown with a 13th-round victory in this 1982 title fight in Las Vegas*

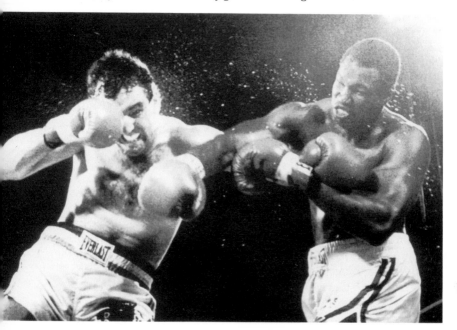

his face with the knuckle part of the glove. If his head was not there to stop the punch your fist would go right across him. It comes in on something of an arc like the left hook and you can increase the shock of impact by a slight downward screwing of the wrist as you land. Don't forget to keep your chin tucked behind your left shoulder and your left glove up protecting your own head.

Pro-tip: Practise in front of a full-length mirror throwing a left lead followed instantly by the right cross. Make sure that your left returns to a guarding position and is on 'red alert' to deliver the *next* punch. Time and again I see boxers connect with the old one-two and then stand back and admire their handiwork. If you want to be the *complete* boxer you must be ready to follow on with your next punch the second your right cross has crashed home.

The Straight Right

The straight right is similar to the right cross but comes straight from the shoulder and the final effect is of going 'through' rather than 'across' your opponent's head. This is one of the most powerful shots in boxing but if you get it wrong it can get you into all sorts of trouble.

You must be sure to create the opening before releasing the punch because it takes a lot of your energy if you miss and it also leaves you wide open to an attack from any opponent who is quick with counter-punches. It is best employed as a counter-punch against an opponent moving in on you and it should follow a left jab or feint. Only in extreme circumstances would you lead with the right.

The most successful exponent of the straight right that I have ever seen (and felt!) was Ingemar Johansson, the last European to hold the world heavyweight championship. His straight right was known as 'Ingo's Bingo' and put out the lights of anybody silly enough or unlucky enough to get in the way. I was one of his knock-out victims and can vouch for the fact that it was like getting hit by lightning. He used to paw with his left as a range-finder and then wham! Over would come the right with the full power of his right shoulder behind it. Johansson was a quite ordinary boxer but that straight right of his cancelled everything out and won him the world's greatest boxing prize.

The execution: The power for the straight right is generated by an explosive drive off the back foot which transfers the body weight to the left side at the instant the right fist is being drilled over your opponent's left hand and straight to the head. At the same time there is a dramatic pivot of your hips and right shoulder and if you get it all together the result is a thumping connection.

Screw your fist inwards just before impact so that on connection the palm is facing the floor. If you are to get the knockout power into the punch, it's vital to pivot at the waist and drive off the rear foot. The best area for landing is the point of the chin.

When you first start trying to throw the straight right against a light punchbag, you are likely to be overconscious of the need to get the correct weight distribution, so the punch will not flow naturally. Try to push the weight ratio out of your mind because it should all come together automatically once you have got the left-right, one-two rhythm working fluently. Remember to start off with a left jab as a distance-finder and then follow on quickly with the right.

The ideal way is to punch 'through' the target and then draw the right fist back to its original position guarding the right side of your face. If you are a southpaw, of course, all the same principles apply except you will be using a straight left rather than the right.

The straight right. *The straight right is one of the most dangerous blows in boxing. It is always preceded by a left lead and carries lots of force. Walter McGowan is bang on target here with a straight right against Salvatore Burruni during their world flyweight title fight at Wembley in 1966. It's a peach of a punch that has knocked Burruni off balance and has given Walter the opportunity to follow up with a left hook. Note the way Walter has got his shoulder behind the punch. McGowan was a decisive points winner*

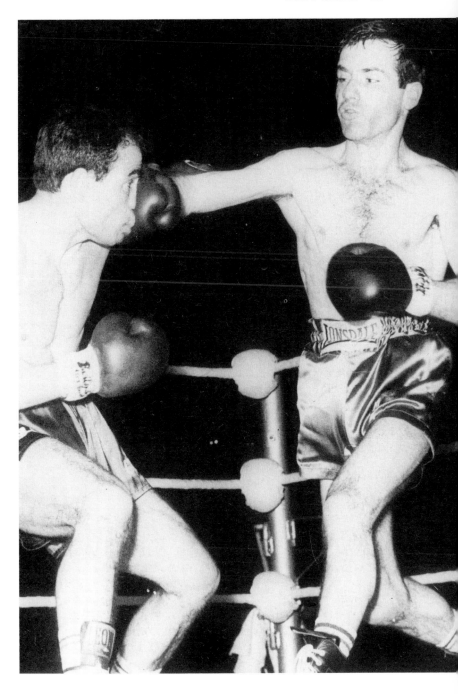

Pro-tip: As with the right cross, too many boxers stand back and admire their handiwork after landing this one-two. I'll pass on a tip I picked up early in my professional career. Once you have thrown the straight right take just half a step backwards as if studying the effect and then come back immediately with a short left hook launched with a swivel of the hips. It means you have turned the traditional old one-two into a one-two-three combination.

I favoured this because the left hook was my most damaging punch. If you feel your right hand is stronger turn the sequence into a left jab, straight right and then – after that short step backwards – a second right to the head. Another effective straight right punch is the one aimed to the body. It is delivered from a crouch with the knees bent and is best drilled in after you have slipped your opponent's left lead. Keep your left hand high guarding your chin because your opponent will be looking for the opportunity to punch down at you.

The Right Uppercut

This is a punch rarely seen in British rings yet it can be a winning blow and should be included in the arsenal of any boxer with ambitions to reach the top. For the greatest effect it should be launched from close quarters or as your opponent comes forward into your punching range. It is particularly effective when suddenly mixed in with a series of straight punches and can stop a fighter in his tracks. An exaggeration of the uppercut is the 'bolo' punch as exhibited by many black fighters including

Moving inside the left jab and countering with a right uppercut to the chin

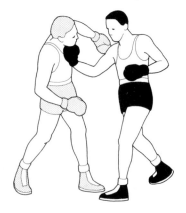

former world welterweight champion Kid Gavilan who used to throw his right on a huge loop before bringing it up and under the defences of his opponents. Gavilan perfected it after working on sugar plantations where he used to cut canes with the bolo knife, hence the name of the punch. The 'bolo' is the sort of punch for which you must have an instinctive feel but the conventional right uppercut can be shaped and sharpened in the gymnasium.

The execution: You need to angle your body slightly to the right with the weight on your right leg and with your right arm in a half-bent position. Swivel from the hip and, with the palm facing up, sweep the right hand up under your opponent's chin or to the body. For the most successful result, you want the connection point of your fist to be the back knuckles and you must meet the target with as much upward force as you can muster. Be careful to keep your left hand back guarding your face because if your uppercut misses it will leave you exposed to a counterattack, particularly from a hooking specialist. Do your best to disguise your intentions as an alert opponent will step back as you throw the uppercut and so, if the punch misses its target, will be in a strong position to launch his own attack. Similar rules apply when throwing a left uppercut – a rare punch from an orthodox boxer. The most effective left uppercut I have ever seen was the punch that Azumah Nelson threw to knock out Pat Cowdell in the first round of their 1985 World featherweight title fight. It was a classic punch with perfect delivery and full follow-through. Nelson brought it up from below hip level and Cowdell didn't see it coming.

Pro-tip: The uppercut is best employed against a bulldozing, shorter opponent who comes in at you with his head lowered. Sway outside his jab and bring the uppercut on an upward path to his body or his chin. Your left hand should be held in a position to guard your face or follow up with a hook. Use the uppercut sparingly because if your opponent starts to anticipate it he could cause you a lot of problems by making you miss. I used to find it most effective when I had an opponent 'going'. With his senses scattered he would be following instincts and taking defensive action to block conventional punches. It was then that a surprise uppercut paid big dividends.

Combinations

Once you have mastered each of the punches that I have outlined you must then concentrate on putting them together in combinations. It's a bit like being a beginner at the piano. First of all you learn one note at a time, then you start to play scales, and finally you work up to being able to play a complete arrangement of notes with both hands. It's the same in boxing but you're hitting an opponent instead of keys! Oh yes, and the piano doesn't try to hit you back.

As in piano playing, timing is all important. But it's not something you can learn from reading this or any other boxing instruction book. It will only come with practice. Plenty of practice. Of course there are the geniuses of the game like Muhammad Ali, Sugar Ray Robinson, Sugar Ray Leonard and Barry McGuigan to whom the timing of punch delivery came naturally. But most fighters have to manufacture their rhythm by working hard in the gymnasium until they are throwing punches in fluent clusters. Former world heavyweight king Floyd Patterson, who had the fastest hands of all my opponents, sharpened his combinations by throwing punches at a heavy punchbag that had an outline of the top half of a human body painted on it. There were seven numbers on the bag: one for the chin, two for the heart, three for the liver, four for the ribs, five for the nose, six for the solar plexus and seven for the temple. His manager Cus D'Amato – Mike Tyson's former mentor – used to shout sequences of numbers and Patterson would launch punches at the numbered areas as fast as D'Amato could call them.

The more varied combinations you have in your repertoire the less predictable you will be in the ring and the harder you will be to beat. You must keep practising them until they become part of a natural pattern. There are dozens of combinations for all situations and these are among those that I would recommend you trying to introduce into your training programme:

Postman's knock: The easiest of all the combinations – a simple double left lead (right for the southpaw) that lands to the head with a rat-a-tat rhythm. It can be used just as effectively whether going forward or on the retreat.

A winning combination. *Sonny Liston is seen here delivering the final combination that knocked out Floyd Patterson in the first round of their world heavyweight title fight in Las Vegas in 1963. The booming right cross has dazed Patterson and now Liston is starting a finishing left uppercut from just below his hips. It swept up through Patterson's guard and landed on the point of his jaw, sending him crashing on to his back. Just look at the position of Liston's right shoulder as the penultimate punch goes* through *the target. The second picture (right) was taken just a split second later and shows that Liston has swung his shoulders back as he prepares to deliver the left with tremendous upward force. Ideally, Liston's right hand should be up guarding his face as he throws the left but he knew that Patterson was on his way out. Experienced big punchers instinctively know when an opponent is ready to be taken out of a fight*

Upstairs, downstairs: This is the most basic yet also one of the most effective combinations. It involves throwing a punch to the body and then switching with the same fist to the head. It can be two stiff jabs or, my particular favourite, a left hook to the ribs followed by an instant left hook to the jaw. If you are accurate enough with the first punch it should make your opponent briefly drop his guard, leaving a gap for the second shot. You can also perform it in reverse, with a left to the head followed by a left to the body. Your weight should be on your front foot as you land and it will add to the overall effect if you take half a pace forward as you deliver the follow-up punch.

The old one-two: The oldest combination in the book but still one of the best. Measure with the left lead and then follow with a fast straight right or right cross, with a pivot of the right shoulder and hip and your weight coming off the back foot onto the front. If you're a southpaw, find the range with your right hand and then whip through with the left.

The old one–two – left jab
followed by a straight right

The old one-two-plus: This is the old one-two as above but with an added left hook or right cross – depending on which is your stronger punch. It is best to add the 'plus' punch only after you have thrown several conventional one-twos. Take a half step back as if this is just the traditional one-two and then suddenly move back in with either a left hook or right cross.

The triple lead: Throw three fast left jabs and then a straight right to the chin. The danger with this sequence is that you tend to finish square on and so are exposed to punches from your opponent. Keep your chin tucked in behind your left shoulder and be prepared to seek the safety of a clinch after throwing the right. This combination is best employed against a tiring opponent who is not perhaps sufficiently alert to take advantage of your square-on position after the final right has been released.

Hook off the jab: I covered this combination in the section on the left hook but it's well worth repeating because it can be a fight-winner. Throw the left lead and then, as you take a pace forward, turn the following punch from an apparent jab into a whiplash hook to the head. If you release the second punch quickly enough it should travel and land out of your opponent's line of vision.

Double hook off the jab: Now we're beginning to get ambitious. Throw a fast jab to the head, then bend to the left and throw a left hook to the body and finish by straightening up and launching a left hook to the chin. Each punch should land with increasing power and your weight distribution should gradually shift from the leading foot to the right leg. Another version of the same combination is a left jab to the head, left hook to the head and then left hook to the body. When you first practise this combination on the bag do it almost at action-replay slow-motion speed and gradually quicken it up when you feel you have the co-ordination and technique right. Once you are doing it properly the sequence of punches should last just a blinking of an eye. It's crucial that you keep your right fist high at the side of your face as protection during this combination. I shall give you another reminder of this in the section on defence.

The left hook and straight right: Slip inside your opponent's lead and drill a left hook to the body followed immediately by a pivot at the waist and a straight right to the chin. This can be equally effective in reverse with a straight right to the body from a crouching position followed by a left hook to the chin over your opponent's right hand.

Jab-uppercut-double-hook: Walk in behind a left jab, fire a right uppercut to the chin, then a left hook to the body followed immediately by a left hook to the head. It sounds easy when putting it down on paper but putting it into operation requires loads of patience and, of course, hours of practice. Be careful not to telegraph the uppercut and I don't advise its use if your opponent has a strong left hook counter because you leave an inviting gap when bringing the right down ready for the upward thrust.

Jab-straight right-left-hook-uppercut-hook: I've saved the most advanced combination for last. You start with an old-fashioned one-two, a jab followed by a straight right off a powerful turn of the right shoulder. Then take half a step forward and throw a left hook to the side of the head, a right uppercut straight through the middle of your opponent's guard to the chin and finally a repeat left hook to the head which should be landed with every ounce of power going into your back knuckles which must be screwed into the landing area.

There are many more combinations that can be built on to the foundation of those that I have featured here depending on your personal range of punches. Remember that every punch you throw in a combination cannot be a full-blooded blow, otherwise you will never get your weight balance right for the following punches.

I always found it best to start the sequence with fairly light, distance-finding punches and then I would gradually increase the power, with the final punch hopefully being the *coup de*

Doing what comes naturally. *This is an interesting picture in that it shows that I used to instinctively throw combinations. Dick Richardson has just gone down to be counted out in our British and Commonwealth heavyweight title fight at Wembley Arena in 1963. The final punch was a left hook to the jaw but the cameraman has snapped me throwing a right cross that hit through thin air where Dick's chin would have been. If he had stayed up, I was all set to fire in another left hook. I was just doing what comes naturally to any boxer who has worked hard enough and long enough in putting together combination punches during training in the gymnasium*

grâce. Most of my combinations used to finish with my good old faithful left hook. Decide for yourself how to put your combinations together, if possible saving your strongest punch for the climax. But remember that you need to have your defence in good shape at the end of the combination and if you are an orthodox boxer you will find that finishing with a right-hand punch could leave you square-on and open to a counter attack.

Pro-tip: Work out your combinations during shadow boxing and while sparring in front of a full-length mirror, then try them out on a punchbag and speed ball before asking a partner (preferably a coach or trainer) to work with you in the ring while he wears the coaching pads for target practice. Don't tense up while throwing your sequence of punches. The more relaxed you are the easier it will be to get the timing and co-ordination right. Give particular attention to the position of your feet when practising your combinations. If your weight balance is wrong at the start it will throw the rest of the sequence out of synchronization. Speed of delivery is essential but, when practising, concentrate first on getting the technique right. The most effective combinations are usually those where you switch the point of attack from head to body or vice versa. Introduce as much variety into your punching as possible but always remember to keep the jab on call for bread-and-butter points scoring.

Counter-Punching

There is, in my opinion, no finer sight in boxing than a skilled counter-puncher at work. It is truly the Noble Art when you see a master of boxing drawing an opponent's lead, slipping it and then countering with his own punches.

Countering is the art of turning defence into attack. The smart counter-puncher appears to give the initiative to his opponent but is actually drawing him into a web ready for the sting. If you can lure an opponent forward and then land your punches while he is on the attack it doubles the power at the moment of impact because of his forward momentum. Sugar Ray Leonard was a master of the counter-punch, zipping his two-fisted shots in after making his opponents miss with subtle slipping and weaving.

The left hook counter. *There have been few better counter punchers than Sugar Ray Leonard. Here's a marvellous illustration of his skill. He has slipped a left lead from Tommy Hearns and has fired a whiplash left hook counter against Tommy's nose. Leonard was rarely content to throw just one punch and you can see that his right is cocked ready to be thumped into the inviting rib cage area. Leonard won this 1981 world welterweight title fight when the referee intervened to save Hearns from further punishment in the 14th round*

The secret of counter-punching lies in accurate timing and anticipation of your opponent's intentions. All the punches I have outlined in this chapter can be employed as counters but instead of leading with them you wait for your opponent to make the first move before unloading your ammunition. There are dozens of methods of countering, among them:

Blocking: You block your opponent's jab with an open right glove and instantly reply with your own left jab. The most common type of block is that of an open glove against your opponent's jab. However, other effective methods of blocking include the use of the shoulder by raising and turning it against the jab, or using the elbow against a body punch by turning your body to meet the blow. If mastered, the art of blocking punches can pave the way for successful counter-punches of your own.

Blocking or catching the jab in the palm of the glove

Blocking with the outside of the glove and countering with the jab

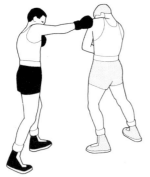

Blocking a straight right by raising the left shoulder and tucking in the chin

Blocking the hook by turning the body to meet the punch on the elbow

Parrying: This is a fencing phrase for warding off the thrust of a blade. In boxing terms to parry means that you deflect your opponent's leading punch and then counter. You can deflect a jab over your left shoulder by pushing the palm of your right

Parry and counter. '*Brown Bomber*' *Joe Louis* (left) *parries a left lead from Jersey Joe Walcott and counters with a left to the body. Louis has pushed Walcott's left down with the palm of his right glove and is now ready to drive his right into Walcott's ribs. The parry-and-counter skill takes split-second timing and you must ensure that you are in range to make contact when you throw your counter. The danger is that after parrying you can fall short with your reply and so leave yourself open to counters to your counters!*

Outside parry of the jab

Outside parry or deflection of the jab by pushing down the opponent's arm, thus forcing him off balance

Inside parry of the jab enabling a
left hand counter punch

Inside parry of the right hand
enabling a straight right counter

glove against your opponent's left glove as he leads. Then throw your own left jab or take a step forward and, with a pivot of the hips and left shoulder, launch a left hook to the chin. Alternatively, you can step to the left as the lead is released and ward off the punch by pushing it over your right shoulder with the outside of your right glove and at the same time countering with a left.

Slipping: This calls for a high degree of skill, a lot of confidence and split-second timing. With a finely judged sideways move of the head you slip inside or outside your opponent's lead and both your hands are free to counter with any of the punches I have already described. By slipping inside the lead, you can get into a particularly good position for a double left hook, first to the body and then the head. Many black American boxers, copying Muhammad Ali and Sugar Ray Leonard, have their hands held down by their hips ready to counter as they go into the slipping routine. But it's not a style I would recommend unless you have naturally nimble footwork and complete confidence in your ability to slip a punch.

I was brought up to believe that you should have a guard up to your face as often as possible and I still think it should be a golden rule unless you happen to have been blessed with a natural gift for timing and body co-ordination. Only you and your trainer can decide which style suits you but be very careful about adopting the hands-down-at-the-side fighting fashion popularized by Muhammad Ali. You've got to be very special to get away with it.

Slipping outside the left jab enabling either a right hook counter to the chin or a short right to the body

Slipping inside the left jab enabling a left hook counter

Slipping outside the left jab and countering with a short left to the body

Slipping inside the left jab and countering with a straight right to the body

Slipping inside the left jab and countering with a straight right

Swaying: Simply sway back from the hips out of range of your opponent's lead and then sway back and let your counterpunches go. You must be sure of your footing to make this work, with your rear foot anchored firmly to the canvas. Deliver your punches with your weight transferred to your front foot.

Leaning or swaying towards the left, away from the left jab, and countering with a straight right to the body

Swaying back from the right hand punch, then countering with the left hook

Ducking: As your opponent leads, duck under the jab by bending the knees and – with your hands held high – go into a crouch from where you will be able to launch a hooking attack to the body.

Ducking under a left jab by bending the knees but keeping the chin protected

Ducking and countering. *Former British and European welterweight champion Peter Waterman, late brother of* Minder *star Dennis, was a superb box-fighter. Here is a fine example of his skill against one of the greats of the ring, 'Cuban Hawk' Kid Gavilan, at Harringay Arena in 1956. Peter has ducked under Gavilan's right and countered with a beautiful straight right to the body. This sort of attack takes courage, split-second timing and a lot of practice in the gym. You must sway at the hips, bend your knees, duck your head and prepare to throw your punch all in the same concerted effort. It's difficult to get it all together and you need to perfect the move before trying it in the ring. In this particular fight, Waterman was awarded a hotly disputed 10-rounds points decision*

Drawing the lead: Draw your opponent off balance by leaning back from the waist and as his lead drops short snap back quickly with your own left. Barry McGuigan was a master at this move, particularly after drawing his opponent's right and then slamming a left hook to the body.

Bobbing and weaving: Drop into a crouch behind a high guard and keep your head bobbing up and down and from side to side as if it's on a spring. Weave inside your opponent's punches and then unload combinations to the head and body. This is a particularly suitable method of counter-punching for stocky fighters who may be having to give away reach advantage. At his peak, there was nobody to touch Smokin' Joe Frazier for this style of fighting. His speciality was to weave inside an opponent's right-hand punch and then smash a short left hook to the unguarded chin. Mike Tyson also mastered these tactics.

Rolling: You roll your head under a punch rather than duck before unleashing your counter, bending forward at the knees and waist. You can also roll against the ropes, maintaining a high guard and then countering after you have made your opponent miss. But this is a highly risky business and you've got to be an accomplished fighter to be able to pull it off, rolling with your opponent's punches so that they fall short of their target. Joe Erskine, former British and Commonwealth heavyweight champion and a great old rival of mine, was a master of rolling on the ropes and of making you miss and then scoring with counter-punches.

In the second half of his career Muhammad Ali used to rest against the ropes, protecting himself behind a high guard and letting his opponents punch themselves out. It was a tactic that worked to perfection in his 1974 world title fight against George Foreman in Zaire. He catapulted off the ropes in the eighth round and knocked out the exhausted Foreman with a classical straight right counter to the jaw. But let me stress that Ali and Erskine were exceptions. My advice to any young boxer would be: stay away from the ropes ... you could get hung. But it's well worth practising the rolling-on-the-ropes and countering technique in the gymnasium so that you are prepared should you get trapped on the ropes during a contest.

Infighting. *Infighting is used to weaken your opponent by effective body punches. There have been few fighters to match Gene Fullmer (left) for being able to bull through defences. Here he has bobbed and weaved his way inside Sugar Ray Robinson's right cross and is about to pound away to the body from close range. You must keep your guard high and your head low, yet at the same time remember not to take your eyes off your opponent. The way Fullmer has forced his way inside here, he is ideally placed to throw a right hook over Robinson's lowered left arm. Fullmer won this 1961 fight on points over 15 rounds to retain his world middleweight title*

The cross counter: Cross counters, either with the right or left, are two of the most punishing blows a boxer can deliver and account for a high percentage of the knock-outs scored. It is best aimed at the point of the chin (or, as old pros say, right on the 'button'). The punch travels across your opponent's arm and over his shoulder in reply to his lead. Get as much shoulder behind your punch as possible when launching either your left hook or right cross, and remember, punch 'through' the target.

Pro-tip: Work with as many different sparring partners as you can find willing to share the ring with you. Your combinations and countering tactics are dictated by the style of your opponent and you need as much gymnasium experience as possible against partners of all shapes, sizes and styles. Remember that the best counters are scored from a foundation of a good defence.

2

The Noble Art of
Self-Defence

Boxing is – or should be – as much about avoiding punches as landing them. Defensive skill is imperative if you are to make any lasting impact in the sport. I have seen a procession of outstanding prospects wrecked because, while great at dishing it out, they have not given enough attention to learning the basic and very necessary art of defending themselves. In the gymnasium, the boxer's workshop, it is vital that you give as much time and effort to defensive tactics as you do to improving your punching.

Think of any of the great champions and you can bet they had a sound defence. It may have been their attacking tactics that took the eye but if you make a close study of their ring strategy you will find they were masters at stopping punches as well as scoring with them. Larry Holmes, for instance, didn't build his impressive record on attack alone. If you get the chance to see any videos of him in action, notice the way he blocks punches with his gloves, keeps a protective guard up when pressing forward and rides punches by clever swaying from the hips.

Mike Tyson is another who grabs the attention with his murderous punching but – although not so obvious to the untrained eye – he is a brilliant exponent of the Noble Art of self-defence. He blocks punches with his gloves and arms, dictates in the clinches with clever smothering tactics and slips and sidesteps punches with a minimum of effort.

I have never been one to condone or encourage the type of boxing where a fighter happily takes three or four punches to land one of his own. In my view the real art of boxing is to hit your opponent without getting hit yourself. You can never give too much time to learning and perfecting the defensive skills among which is the art of covering up. There's the **full cover** that Muhammad Ali used to employ when lying on the ropes. You jack-knife your arms in the middle of your body with your elbows close together at the top of your waistband and you shield your face behind your gloves, just peeping through the middle of them so that you can see what your opponent is doing. The idea is to take as many of his punches as you can on the forearms and gloves. Be ready to twist and turn to lessen the power of the punches that are likely to be thrown round the backs of your elbows in the region of your ribs and kidneys.

Then there's the **half cover**, holding your right glove up to your face, tucking your chin into your left shoulder and placing your left arm across your waist as a protection and also ready as a counter-weapon.

If trapped in a corner, the **cross cover** is a useful defensive ploy. You virtually hug the upper part of your body, with your left arm wrapped around your neck and your right arm wrapped around your rib section. You will be able to get a clear view of your opponent's intentions over your left elbow and then sway, roll and weave to avoid his punches.

These three cover-up positions are extreme forms of defence that should be used if you are under a heavy blitz, particularly on the ropes.

The Importance of Nimble Footwork

While it's the ducking, slipping, blocking, parrying, bobbing and weaving that I outlined in the section on countering that are the basic methods of defensive boxing, the feet are just as important as the hands in defending yourself. Never forget that it is harder to hit a moving target. You must learn to sidestep both to your left and right, and to circle backwards around the ring in both a clockwise and anti-clockwise direction. Any boxer who climbs through the ropes able to move only forwards or backwards in a straight line is courting trouble. You must be able to move quickly out of the line of your opponent's attack and then unload your counter-punches. Most people find it easier to move to their left (or right, if a southpaw). I recommend plenty of fast shadow boxing in the gymnasium against an imaginary opponent until you feel comfortable sidestepping either way.

The sidestep, or shift, is a short, gliding step with a good balance and rhythm maintained throughout the movement. When moving to your left your left foot leads; when moving to your right your right foot leads. It's really quite simple once you start putting it into practice. One vital thing to remember is that your feet should never cross and don't splay your legs too wide. This restricts your mobility and also makes it difficult for you to punch with real power off the front foot. It's no exaggeration when commentators describe boxers as dancing round the ring. By getting up on your toes and using the sort of footwork you see on the dancefloor you can dictate a contest from long range. But try not to be flashy with your footwork. Dancing around unnecessarily can be a waste of precious energy. The greatest champions are usually light and quick on their feet. Sugar Ray Robinson, for instance, used to have a nightclub act in which his rhythmic tap dancing was of a highly professional class.

You will find that if punching correctly your foot movement will be slightly ahead of your hands. It will come naturally to you provided you are getting properly balanced. If you are perfectly balanced, you should not be easily knocked out of your stride, but will be able to move quickly and smoothly in any direction as the situation demands.

Watch any of the top fighters in action and you will see that, without thinking about it, there is a slight foot movement before the delivery of their punches. The hardest punches are those that are delivered as you step in, and with a good defensive strategy you should be looking to step in with counter-punches after making your opponent miss with clever footwork. When moving sideways it's best if you can keep your front foot in line with your opponent otherwise you will be out of distance when countering.

If you are up against a good left hooker most coaches tip that the best defence is to move away from the punch to your left so that your opponent has to reach and is therefore not correctly balanced when throwing it. There's also the school of thought

On your guard. *Sugar Ray Leonard gets himself trapped in a corner by Roberto Duran during their world welterweight title fight in Montreal in 1980. But Leonard has adopted the full-cover defence to restrict Duran's chance of making the most of a critical moment. Leonard is carefully watching Duran through his high guard. The best way out of this sort of tight corner is to try to 'turn' your opponent, waiting for him to put his weight on his front foot and then suddenly sliding across the ropes to make him miss. If you get your timing right his forward momentum should carry him forward into the ropes. Leonard got himself out of this corner but Duran won a narrow points victory*

that says you should move to your right and towards the punch so that he cannot settle to throw it with any great accuracy. This was a tactic that Larry Holmes used with a great degree of success against Gerry Cooney's devastating left hook, cleverly pushing his right glove down into the crook of Cooney's left

The elbow block. *Muhammad Ali cleverly took the majority of George Foreman's thumping blows on the forearms and elbows during their memorable 'Rumble in the Jungle' in Zaire in 1974. Here he uses his right elbow to block an attempted left to the ribs from Foreman. I wouldn't recommend the way Ali lay around on the ropes against Foreman, but if you do find yourself forced into playing 'rope-a-dope' tricks make sure you jack-knife your arms in the middle of your body and keep your gloves high guarding your face. Ali was luring Foreman into a trap the whole time he was lying on the ropes. He allowed the champion to punch himself to the edge of exhaustion and then came catapaulting off the ropes in the eighth round to knock out Foreman with a crashing straight right counter to the head*

arm every time he shaped to throw it. This stopped him getting any leverage for his punch. However, speaking as somebody who relied heavily on the left hook, I have to say I preferred it if my opponent was moving to his right and into my firing line. My advice is that you should move to your left against a left hooker and to your right against an opponent with a strong right. By moving and circling you can nullify your opponent's strongest weapon. But against a swinger step inside so that his punches go over your shoulders or around your head.

But remember when making all these avoiding movements to be prepared to fire counter-punches of your own. Time and again I see boxers expending precious energy making opponents hit and miss but then not cashing in on their defensive work by landing scoring punches.

Defence is just as important at close quarters as at long range. Strictly speaking holding is not allowed but it's one of the tricks of the trade that you need to master if you are going to be a complete fighter. I vividly recall the way Muhammad Ali continually tied me up in the clinches in our world title fight. His arms snapped round me like a steel clamp and then on the instruction from the referee to 'break' he would push my left hand down with his right and then jump back out of reach. Yes, it was illegal – but extremely effective. Hitting and holding is another illegal method of punching. I have to admit I used to get away with it whenever I could, holding on the blind side of the referee and hooking to the head and body with my free hand. There will be boxing purists who will frown on me for passing on these sort of 'dirty tricks' of the trade, but boxing can be rough and tough and you have got to know how to look after yourself in all situations. Try to get your head beneath your opponent's in the clinches and you should be in the driving seat if you can get your arms inside his. Give him as small a target as possible to aim at and if possible work away with both your hands. Even if you are not landing with real power you will at least impress the judges and referee that you are on top and scoring points.

Pro-tip: If you are alert enough you should be able to anticipate when your opponent is going to let his punches go. You can really aggravate him and reduce his punching power by pushing his shoulder or upper arm a split second before he releases his

The cover-up. *Sugar Ray Robinson (left) presents Carmen Basilio with the smallest possible target during their world middleweight title fight at Chicago in 1958. Get into this tucked position if you are under fire, but be prepared to throw punches of your own as soon as your opponent has committed himself. Robinson weathered this storm from the aggressive Basilio to score a 15-rounds points victory and regain the world crown*

punch. This should make his blow fall just short of the intended target. Good defensive boxing takes courage because you have to make sure that your opponent has committed himself to his line of attack before making your protective move.

The quicker your anticipation and the quicker your reflexes the more successful you are going to be. I always found I could 'read' what an opponent was about to do by watching his eyes.

There's a split-second giveaway, with the sort of range-finding eye movement a darts player makes before throwing.

Another defensive tip is that you should always try to keep your right elbow tucked into your side when jabbing with your left (left elbow if you're a southpaw). Floyd Patterson used to shadow box with a rolled newspaper tucked under his right elbow. If it dropped to the floor he knew he was letting his elbow stray too far from his body and so leaving an inviting gap at which an opponent could aim body shots.

3

The Stance

Choosing which stance to adopt in the ring depends on your size, your style and your attitude. If you are tall with a long reach you are best advised to take the classic English upright stance. Stand, left foot foremost, with your feet just a little more than shoulder width apart. Your weight should be evenly distributed with a slight bias towards the back foot so that you have a strong, flexible base. Hold your hands in front of you at shoulder height, with your elbows tucked into your sides just above the waistband. Avoid any tension in the arms because tightened muscles will restrict your punching speed and efficiency. Just loosely clench your fists until you are delivering punches.

Your left shoulder should be half turned to the right with your chin tucked down behind it. By standing side-on the tall boxer will make the most of his reach advantage and the left jab will be his main foundation-laying punch.

If you are short you will adopt a more square-on stance so that you can make two-handed attacks from behind a high guard. Make sure you always keep your chin tucked down because standing square-on you present more of a target to your opponent.

When you have settled on your most comfortable stance, get into the habit of bending your knees slightly so that you feel you have a spring in your legs. This will not only improve your mobility but will also give you extra zip when you are throwing your punches. Try not to be too stiff.

As I have stated earlier, be very wary about adopting the flashy hands-down-by-the-hips style that was perfected and popularized by Muhammad Ali. You need to be a master of slipping and swaying and have excellent footwork to stand any chance of success with this extremely risky method of boxing.

This is the best-known stance in boxing – Muhammad Ali, pictured at his peak. He has got both feet anchored here, but in the ring he was an up-on-the-toes dancer which is the main reason he was rarely a heavy puncher. Ali, until his later years, was invariably on the move and so didn't get full bodyweight behind his punches. The knockout punchers usually have both feet planted on the canvas when launching their heaviest ammunition. Ali – and Sugar Ray Leonard after him – adopted a flashy, hands-down-by-the-hips style that suited him because he had natural rhythm and an instinctive sense of timing. But it is a dangerous method to copy unless you are exceptionally nimble on your feet

I mentioned attitude as being one of the things to take into account when deciding on your stance. Personality and temperament play a big part in a boxer's make-up. You may be the aggressive Mike Tyson type who would benefit from throwing two-fisted attacks from a square-on stance; alternatively you may be a cautious, calculating character best suited to a countering style of boxing. You certainly have to have a special brand of confidence to try to get away with the 'floating-and-stinging' technique of an Ali or a Leonard.

Whatever stance and style you adopt, make sure you remember that it is as important to know how to defend yourself as it is to hit your opponent. Bear this in mind when deciding on your stance so that you are poised to quickly switch from defence to attack or vice versa as the situation demands.

4
The Southpaw

Had I started my boxing career 20 years later it is probable that I would have been a southpaw. My left hand was far and away my strongest and the most natural thing for me would have been to lead with my right and use my left as the follow-up destruction punch. But in my early days southpaws were looked on almost as freaks and I was encouraged to box in the orthodox, left foot forward style. Southpaws are common – and very successful – in the modern ring and many have gone right to the top. Without pausing for thought I find it easy to name Marvin Hagler, Maurice Hope, Jim Watt, Alan Minter, Cornelius Boza-Edwards, Herol Graham, Brian Curvis, Dave Charnley, Chris Finnegan, Richard Dunn, Freddie Gilroy, Johnny Caldwell, Charlie Nash, Jackie Paterson, Jack Bodell and Karl Mildenberger who made it to championship status while leading with their right fists.

Dick McTaggart, 1956 Olympic lightweight gold medallist and one of Britain's most successful amateur boxers, was another southpaw who found putting his right foot and right fist forward was the right way for a winning career. McTaggart was a master at counter-punching and was brilliant at deceiving opponents with crafty feints and clever footwork.

The term 'southpaw' originates from baseball. In the main baseball stadiums in America the right-handed pitcher (equivalent to the bowler in cricket) pitches from east to west, so his throwing arm is on the north side of the ground. If he is a left-handed pitcher, then his throwing hand (or paw) is to the south – hence the name.

The southpaw should concentrate on perfecting his feinting and countering techniques because he tends to have most success when drawing an orthodox boxer's lead and then letting his own punches go. Tommy Hearns made the fatal error of

A model craftsman. *Here's a superb study of former world middleweight champion Marvin Hagler in aggressive action. He is beautifully balanced as he throws a right hook. His left glove is guarding his chin, his elbow protects his ribs and he is all set to throw a left cross as part of a classic combination. Any southpaws reading this book could not have a finer craftsman on which to model themselves*

leading against Marvin Hagler in their 1985 world middleweight championship match and walked onto some of the most savage counter-attacks I have ever seen.

If you are a southpaw, make sure you get plenty of practice at blocking and avoiding straight rights and left hooks from left-leading sparring partners because these are the two main punches with which orthodox opponents try to blast your defence. Move in an anti-clockwise direction to your right, circling away from the strong right hand carried by most orthodox boxers but keep your right hand high to guard against the left hook.

Pro-tip: Southpaws and orthodox boxers can learn from this advice. When sparring in the gym, practise what is known as the forward shift – switching your stance, southpaw to orthodox or vice versa. It's a manoeuvre that can confuse your opponent but only bring it into play in an emergency. Don't overplay the shift otherwise you could finish up confusing yourself even more than your opponent. Just use it as a surprise tactic.

5

Your Opponent

Your ring strategy will obviously be dictated to a great extent by your opponent's size and style. It's important to get to know as much as you possibly can about your rival before you step into the ring. This isn't easy in the amateur ranks but do as much homework on your opponent as possible, and at least find out about his style.

This is the 'Video Age' as far as top professional boxers are concerned and they now go to great lengths to study the opposition. Barry McGuigan, for instance, has a library of video tapes on every leading featherweight and junior lightweight fighter in the world. He got to know Eusebio Pedroza inside out by studying video replays of his fights before their classic world championship match in London in 1985. It wasn't just luck that Barry was able to avoid Pedroza's dangerous right counters. He had worked out his tactics in advance and completely out-thought the veteran champion thanks to careful pre-fight planning and preparation.

If your opponent is considerably taller than you, it will prob-ably mean that you concede reach advantage. He will no doubt be looking to make the most of his reach by keeping you on the end of a long jab. This is where any gymnasium practice you have put in on the skill of slipping a lead will pay dividends. You must try to slip inside his lead and counter to the head and body as you move in, and then stay there at close quarters, banging away with short, jolting punches that will bring him down to size.

If you are having difficulty slipping the lead make sure you keep on the move, switching direction as often as possible so that you do not present him with an easy target for his jabs. Try to cut down his ring space by driving him into corners and cutting the angles. Remember that you can duck under a lead

Do your homework. *Barry McGuigan is a real hunter of a fighter. He stalks his opponents and softens them up with whiplash left hooks to the body, sometimes perilously close to the borderline. There has rarely been a boxer better at doing his homework than Barry. He gets to know his opponents inside out by studying video film of them in action. This is why he is so often a move and a thought ahead of his opponents. A classic example was his defeat of Eusebio Pedroza (left) when he took the Panamanian's world featherweight title with a magnificent points victory at Queen's Park Rangers football ground in 1985. He cleverly foxed Pedroza into thinking he had only his left hook to worry about while all the time in secret training sessions he had been sharpening his right. This picture shows Barry threatening Pedroza with his left hand in the seventh round. The champion moved to his left as Barry knew he would, and a split second after this picture was taken he unleashed a right that dropped the startled Pedroza and swung the fight heavily in Barry's favour. Always try to keep a trick up your sleeve. Don't put all you have to offer on show in the first round*

Nowhere to hide. *Tommy Hearns had height and reach advantage against Marvin Hagler in their world middleweight title showdown in Las Vegas in 1985, but Hagler gave him no room in which to manoeuvre and cut down his ring space by driving him into corners and cutting his angles. Hearns has managed to slip this right lead from Hagler but he has nowhere to hide and, within seconds of this third-round picture being taken, he had been driven back on to the ropes and knocked out with a stunning volley of punches. I could not understand the tactics that Hearns adopted in this contest. He chose to fight rather than box and this, of course, was playing right into the rough, tough hands of Hagler. If you are up against a shorter, harder punching opponent try to make full use of your reach and height advantage by keeping exchanges at long range. But try not to follow a predictable path around the ring, and keep your jab pumping out to stop him from composing himself for a hard-hitting attack*

as well as slip it, or block it. The hardest thing of all if you have a big reach disadvantage is to counter and you will need fast hands as well as quick footwork if you are to get inside and counter to the head and body.

Whenever I met a taller opponent I used to quickly sink left hooks into the belly to discourage him from picking me off from long range behind a high guard. My objective was to make him bring his guard down and then counter over the top of his lead. Those body shots usually had the desired effect of making him want to hang on in clinches while getting his breath back. This meant I had nullified his reach advantage and it gave me the opportunity to work away at close quarters.

The best form of defence in the ring is often – but not always – attack. If you are under heavy fire it sometimes pays to tuck your chin down and to start throwing leather from all angles. Only you can decide when this positive policy is likely to pay off, but if you are being outsmarted it just might work in your favour if you try to change the pattern of the fight by suddenly forcing the pace.

If you are up against a bobbing, weaving shorter opponent who comes at you out of a crouch you should be looking to meet him with a stiff jab and a follow-up right uppercut.

He will be trying to get in to close quarters, but if you are the superior boxer don't get drawn into a slugging match. Keep that left jab pumping out, even if only to knock him off balance and so prevent him from composing himself ready for a two-fisted attack. Don't follow a predictable path around the ring if he's charging after you. Side-step to the left and right and then, when you've got him wrong-footed, dart in with a quick battery of punches before getting back 'on your bike' and moving around the ring at speed. Puzzle him as much as possible with the variety and invention of your moves. This sort of aggressive, all-action fighter causes most damage if you present him with a sitting target. So keep on the move and irritate the hell out of him with that left jab, and let your combinations go when you know he can't trap you into a close-quarter exchange. Force him on to his back foot as often as possible because he likes to have his weight on his front foot for the launching of his heaviest punches. Above all, don't fight him. *Box* him.

If your opponent is a wild swinger just stay cool and watch for the swings being launched. Swingers give prior warning of their intent because they send their fist on a circular tour. The moment they set themselves to let the punch go step smartly inside and land a telling blow on what will be an unguarded target.

While you are landing quick, straight punches his blows should be hitting thin air around the back of your neck. You can also step out of range of the swings but make sure you have your chin tucked into your shoulder and your guard held high. I often see boxers making the mistake of stepping back out of range of swinging punches with their chins held out. The punch sometimes just clips them but it is enough to scatter their senses and put them on the road to defeat. If you do get caught like this, try to manoeuvre into a clinch while your head clears.

If you get trapped on the ropes go into one of the cover-up stances that I described in the Noble Art of Defence section and take the first opportunity to 'turn' your opponent; that is draw him forward while you have your back to the ropes and then suddenly sidestep and steer him onwards with your left or right glove so that he is confronted with the ropes while you are on your way to the centre of the ring.

Make it your aim to stay in the centre of the ring, forcing your opponent to use a lot of territory (and energy) while attempting to land his swings. Back him up as often as you can so that he can't get his weight on to his front foot. The odds are that he will tire himself out if you are making him miss more times than he lands. Whatever you do, keep calm and think out your moves.

When you tangle with a smart counter-puncher try not to lead. A counter-puncher usually likes to box off his back foot, so draw him forward and try to 'con' him into leading and then throw your own counters.

Never ever try to delude yourself in the ring. Make quick and honest judgements and then adjust your strategy to suit the situation. If you know you are outgunned or up against a more skilful opponent, accept it and work out tactics that will keep you in the contest with a victory chance.

You could, for instance, find yourself matched with a counter-puncher who is too smart for you when you try to draw him into leading. Accept that it's pointless trying to play him at his countering game and adopt an attacking role but keep your guard high and get in and out as quickly as possible before he can get into top gear with his counter-attack.

Listen to what you are told in the corner between rounds because the men looking after you have the advantage of being able to see the fight from a wide angle. Your cornermen are your extra eyes. Go by what they see and what they say. Their instructions could help you turn a possible defeat into a victory.

Outstanding ring generals will often deliberately make a conscious effort to get close to their corner during a round so that they can hear what instructions their advisers are shouting out.

Corner coaching is, of course, not allowed while a round is in progress but I promise you that it goes on all the time at all levels of the game. You will also find experienced ringmasters manoeuvring opponents towards their own corner near the end of each round so that they don't have to waste energy walking to their stool when the bell goes. This won't help a three-round amateur too much, but if you are in a ten-round contest it can certainly save the legs and your opponent will find himself having a lot of walking to do.

There is an old boxing saying that 'right is might' against a southpaw and you will often hear ringside supporters advising an orthodox boxer to throw the right when he is fighting a 'wrong-way-round' opponent. Well, I always found that a left hook was just as rewarding a punch to use as a right against the southpaw opponents that I met, including, in championship contests, Karl Mildenberger and Jack Bodell.

It's wisest for an orthodox boxer to circle clockwise around the ring and away from his southpaw opponent's usually more powerful left hand. Carry the left hand high and keep the chin tucked in to guard against right hooks. Look to slip inside his right lead or duck under it and counter with a left hook. You can also parry his right jabs with your left hand and throw a quick right counter.

Pro-tip: If you get advance notice that your opponent is going to be a southpaw and you cannot find a right-foot/right-hand-forward sparring partner, ask your trainer to don practice pads and adopt a southpaw stance. Practise moving in a clockwise direction and slip inside and outside the right lead. Familiarize yourself as much as possible with facing the right hand as the leading punch so that you are accustomed to the 'wrong way round' style that can be really confusing if you do not have experience of facing southpaws.

6

Feinting and Foxing

It pays to be a good liar in the ring. You should continually be trying to convince your opponent that you are about to hit him in a completely different place to where you actually mean to aim your punches. You can use your hands, eyes, shoulders and feet to deceive him into adjusting his defence so that he leaves an opening for your punches. My favourite feint was a pretence at throwing a left hook to the body. I would lower my eyes and just shrug my left shoulder as if about to release a body shot. As my opponent dropped his right hand to block the 'phantom' punch I would let go with a left hook to the jaw. Or you can simply show one hand and throw the other one.

The golden rule about feinting is that you must not use the same trick over and over again, otherwise your opponent will get wise to it and will launch a counter-attack that will not be a fake just as you are going into your feinting routine.

There are dozens of feints that you should practise while shadow boxing in front of a full-length mirror. These are among the more obvious ones that you should master:

(a) Pretend to jab to the head and then quickly follow up with a genuine jab to the body;

(b) Cock the right hand and pull the right shoulder back, a move that can create an opening for a left-hook counter;

(c) Feint a left-right combination to the head and then suddenly turn it into a left-right combination to the body;

(d) Shape as if to throw a left hook to the body and then the head but make your actual punch a right cross to the chin;

(e) Dummy a side-step to the right and then launch an attack from the left.

All these feints can be performed in reverse, and remember, it's not only your fists that you use in 'let's pretend' movements

A feinting master. *Sugar Ray Leonard (left) was a master of feinting and his now-you-see-me-now-you-don't tactics lured many opponents into his counter-punching trap. Here he is leaning back out of range of an attack from another modern master, Roberto Duran. He is now ready to counter with a left-right combination. You need to get your weight quickly off your back foot when thowing your counters. Leonard won this 1980 world welterweight title fight in New Orleans when Duran uncharacteristically retired during the eighth round*

to bemuse and confuse your opponents. A shrug of the shoulder, a simple glance with the eyes, a shift of body weight, a nod of the head, a pivot of the hips and a dummy movement of the feet can all help deceive your opponent into believing you are about to do the opposite to what you really intend.

Feinting plays an important part in defence as well as attack. Just pretending to throw punches could get you off the hook if you are under pressure. You can buy time by setting up a decoy attack while actually putting your main effort into getting out of a tight corner with quick and clever footwork.

Always be looking to fox your opponent into getting the wrong impression of what you are thinking and planning. Sugar Ray Robinson was a master of foxing tactics, pretending he was hurt and letting his defences drop. His opponents would be lured into the trap and as they came forward to take advantage of the situation they would find themselves walking on to violent counter-punches.

Feinting is boxing with the mind as well as the body. You must try to out-think your opponent and, even if you are under severe pressure, never let him believe that he is in complete command unless it's part of a crafty plan to lure him into a feeling of false confidence.

Pro-tip: When practising on the speed ball, wait until you have got a good rhythm going and then try deliberately throwing an occasional pretend punch. You must try to do it without losing your rhythm on the ball. And when shadow boxing, have sessions in which you make all the body movements for throwing punches but without letting a single punch go.

7
Training

Training begins not in the gymnasium but out on the road. It can be a long and lonely road but one that must be taken if you are to gain the kind of super fitness a boxer requires to reach the top and stay there.

A boxing scribe once asked former world heavyweight champion Rocky Marciano what he considered his strongest asset and was surprised when the Rock replied: 'My legs.' Marciano used to spend hours running strength and stamina into his legs and lungs, and was always fit enough to go 20 rounds whenever he put his championship on the line.

Roadwork is, in my opinion, the most vital part of your preparation for boxing, whether you are training for three-round amateur contests or the longer, more demanding professional distances. You can have fast fists and a powerful punch but if your legs and lungs aren't in good condition you will find the going tough when you climb into the ring. The tell-tale sign of somebody who has not done his roadwork is when you see a boxer flat-footed and puffing and blowing. You must be able to get up on your toes both to launch attacks and to take fast evasive action. Swift, strong legs will help you to move in and out and to take yourself away from trouble if under pressure.

If you are a 'townie' I suggest you begin your road running as early as possible in the mornings before the traffic exhaust and fumes start to pollute the air. Don't set out to break any world running records. The objective is to build strength into your legs and condition yourself for the endurance test into which many contests develop. You don't achieve this with one work-out on the road. You must be prepared to go out at least three or four times a week, even when you are not getting into shape for a fight. I promise you that the more work you put in on the road, the easier it will be for you in the ring.

I used to average four or five miles on the road every morning when starting my preparations for a contest and drop it to two or three miles in the last few days before the fight. I was always well wrapped up in a tracksuit, even in the hottest weather, and used to wear heavy army boots so that my old feet would really appreciate the lightness and comfort when I switched to boxing boots. If you are overweight or out of condition take it easy on your first few road runs and gradually build up the distance and the variety of your running.

Remember when you're out running that you are not trying to be the next Seb Coe or Steve Cram. Start at a comfortable jogging pace and gradually increase your speed, mixing in the occasional quick sprint for a hundred metres or so. Run on the balls of your feet, not flat-footed, and try using a high knee action for your quickest sprints.

Don't run in a straight line all the time. Zig-zag and practise side-steps, even running backwards for short bursts provided there is room to manoeuvre without causing interference to pedestrians – and don't take the risk of getting hit by traffic! Shadow box for part of the time as you run, practising combinations and feints.

Interval running becomes more important as you come to the peak of your training programme. With this form of running you will not be looking to put in distance as much as variety. It's handy to do the work on a running track if possible but if not use trees and lamp-posts to measure your distances. You should set out to run a fairly fast 100 metres, then a slower 200 metres followed by a flat-out sprint over 50 metres and then a two-minute jog followed by a repeat of the faster work. Intensified interval running spread over about an hour a day for three weeks of your peak training effort will make your heart pump stronger and give you added energy when fight time arrives. I am being very general with these instructions on interval running because no two boxers follow exactly the same training routine. You need to get coaching advice as to what sort of interval running would suit your physique and stamina requirements.

The coach will take age, weight, build and current fitness into account when planning your schedule. Obviously a boxer training for a 12-round contest is going to need a different training programme to the amateur preparing for a three-round bout. But the principle is the same. You must get out on the road and run. Some boxers who are natural athletes can run for an hour or more and hardly notice any stress or strain, while many – probably the majority – find the roadwork and interval running a real slog. I had to force myself to get out on the road but once I was into a rhythm I used to quite enjoy it. In fact, I can honestly say that there's no feeling in the world quite like that of being in tip-top shape after a completed roadwork programme; also, if you are up with the birds, you will come to appreciate that it is the best time of day. Everything you do on the road will help not only build your stamina and endurance but also your self-confidence. An important point to remember is that you should always warm-up for at least five minutes before doing your interval work, otherwise you will risk pulling a muscle. If you are a youngster whose leg muscles have not yet fully developed try not to run on concrete roads because you could risk getting shin splints, an injury caused by heavy pounding. If possible run in a park or through woods.

Many boxers don't like running alone and get a pal to run with them or somebody to accompany them on a bike. It can certainly takes some of the slog out of the roadwork if you have a companion but whatever you do don't turn your running into a competition. Put in the work that you need to do without trying to prove that you have greater speed or more stamina than your colleague. Leave that to the athletes.

To supplement all the work you do out on the road you should include a rope-skipping routine in every gymnasium session. The roadwork helps you build reserves of stamina, while fast rope skipping helps you develop agility and balance and gets your hands, trunk and legs moving in synchronization. One of the best rope-skippers I ever saw was former world heavyweight champion Sonny Liston, who was as light on his feet as a ballet dancer despite weighing around 16 stone. He used to skip to music to help him with his rhythm and I recommend it as a good idea to help you get into a smooth skipping routine. Try to keep your body relaxed while skipping and vary the pattern of your leg movements, skipping with your feet together and then with alternate 'one leg' skips while balanced on the balls of your feet. Increase the speed of the rope turn and keep changing direction, skipping while going backwards and forwards. Don't look down at your feet and perfect the cross-arm rope-turning technique. Some people seem to think that skipping is a girlish thing to do, but it is a vital part of a boxer's preparation and, done properly, can be extremely satisfying.

Try to get an hour or so's rest after your roadwork and, of course, don't run, train or fight on a full stomach. It should be at least another five hours before you go into the gymnasium for your 'indoor' work. Don't make the mistake of hanging around there for hours. It is much better to get your training compressed into a maximum 90-minute session rather than spread it out with long pauses in between each work section. I hesitate to offer the sort of advice on exercises that you find in some boxing books because no two boxers follow the same training routine (although there again a lot of amateurs do and that is why we tend to turn out so many stereotyped boxers who lack individual flair and invention). I prefer to speak in general terms and recommend that you and your trainer work out a training schedule to suit your personal requirements. You should include exercises that help not only your fitness but also your skill. Too many boxers put all their concentration into building their strength and stamina and forget that even if they are in championship class there are still skills that need to be improved. I suggest the following as a fairly basic gymnasium schedule for a boxer in the early part of his training programme for a three-round amateur contest, the routine starting at, say, 6.00 pm:

6.00 pm: General warm-up exercises (running on the spot, shadow boxing, skipping, all-round muscle-suppling exercises). Work up a light sweat and keep moving rhythmically about until your muscles feel nice and relaxed. If you're making weight wear a heavy woollen tracktop and bottoms or a special plastic weight-reducing suit. Even if you're not trying to reduce your poundage it's imperative that you keep warm at all times and you should have a track top to pull on between routines.

6.10 pm: Shadow box in front of a full-length mirror, practising your punch combinations, feints and defensive moves. If possible have your trainer watch you so that he can point out any mistakes that you are making. Use your imagination and convince yourself that there's an opponent in front of you. Look carefully to see if you are telegraphing any of your punches. The more disguise and deception you can introduce into your moves the better.

6.20 pm: Work out on the heavy punchbag for four two-minute rounds, concentrating particularly on the straight jab and then switching to two-fisted attacks to the 'head' and 'body' of the bag. Let the bag swing into you before releasing your punches and occasionally feint and deliberately hold your punch back and sidestep as the bag comes towards you.

Punch from the shoulder and really sink the gloves into the bag. Try not to be lazy and predictable with your punches. In your mind that bag has got to represent your indestructible opponent and you should be trying to vary your punches to master him. Move about on your feet as if you are in the ring and put thought and style into every move. Have a short

---

Swing the bag. *When you are working with the heavy bag, imagine you are facing an opponent. Get the bag swinging so that you can get mobility into your work. Occasionally feint and deliberately hold your punch back and sidestep as the bag comes towards you. Don't be lazy when working with the bag. Practise combinations and treat it as a sparring partner which is not going to hit back*

breather in between each two-minute session, taking deep breaths and keeping your muscles loose with arm shaking and light leg-loosening movements.

6.32 pm: Four two-minute rounds on the speedball, maizeball or standball. Now you have really got to work at timing your punches. Speed of punch is essential on each of these balls and you need to get a rhythm as well as power into your combinations. If you are working with the standball, try circling both ways as it comes towards you and practise and perfect your

---

Quickness and quality. *Hand speed is all important in the ring and you can sharpen the quickness and the quality of your punches by working on the speedball. Here we see former world heavyweight title challenger Gerry Cooney at work on the speedball. To encourage him, his trainer has painted slogans on the ball – 'hard work pays' and 'keep punching'. When working on the speedball make sure you get rhythm as well as power into your punches*

counters with either hand. You will sometimes stand flat-footed when working on the speedball but when training with the other balls make sure you are on the move and slide your feet in as you deliver your punches. The speedball, the ball suspended from a platform, is to be used to get co-ordination between hand and eye. It's all about speed and rhythm.

6.44 pm: Three two-minute and three three-minute rounds of sparring, preferably against two or three different sparring partners. It sometimes pays to spar with somebody much lighter than you to help increase your speedwork (obviously hold back on your punches) and work with somebody heavier than yourself

---

Laying the foundation. *Sparring is the most important part of a boxer's preparation for boxing. Muhammad Ali – or young Cassius Clay as he is here – used to have a team of four or five sparring partners lined up to give him work outs of up to 20 rounds a session. While he would often clown for the purposes of publicity, Ali treated his sparring with deadly seriousness. It's while sparring that you lay the foundation for all your ring movements and punch combinations. Remember, you don't spar to prove yourself the king of the gym. The objective is to improve co-ordination, polish moves and increase the all-round accuracy and quality of your punches . . . and, of course, to get you fit for the rigours of the 'real' ring*

to help increase your strength particularly in the close-quarter exchanges.

Practise your moves and tactics against a variety of opponents and, if possible, against a partner with a similar style to the one you are to meet in your next contest. It is essential that you wear a headguard, a gumshield and heavy gloves to reduce all risks of injury. Extra rounds of sparring can be added against your coach who can use large pad-gloves to help you with your combinations, counters and feints.

7.03 pm: A hard session of ground exercises, including sit-ups, press-ups, squat thrusts and squat jumps, bench jumps, step ups, neck rolls, burpees (leg shoots from a crouching position) and dorsal raise (lying on your front with your legs held and raising your head and shoulders off the floor with your hands clasped at the back of your neck); also work with the medicine ball to strengthen your stomach muscles. These are all explosive muscle-strengthening exercises and should be performed under trainer supervision as a carefully worked-out circuit programme. Circuit training involves linking a series of exercises together and repeating each exercise a set number of times. The objective is to build up strength in the arms, legs, stomach and neck. It's essential that you get specialist advice before embarking on your exercise programme.

7.20 pm: Muscle-loosening wind-down exercises. Nothing strenuous. Just ten minutes of relaxed movements to help you warm-down. Then straight into a shower and remember to wrap up well when you leave the gymnasium. The best-trained sportsmen are particularly susceptible to colds at this time.

Professional boxers should have a similar routine but add about five minutes to each section, with three-minute rounds on all the gymnasium equipment. The professional should also pay more attention to stamina exercises.

Be very careful if you are going to use weights. Weight-training can be beneficial under the correct supervision but weight-*lifting* can be disastrous. You rarely see a successful boxer with a heavily muscled body. You need loose, supple muscles to produce fast, powerful punches. It is all about timing rather than strength, and heavy muscles tend to restrict a boxer's mobility. By all means use weights in your training but I stress again only under the supervision of somebody who knows the difference between weight-training and weight-lifting.

Four training sessions a week in a gymnasium should be sufficient. Vary your exercise routines so that you don't get stale or bored and make sure you don't make the mistake of overtraining. Barry McGuigan couldn't understand why he was feeling exhausted halfway through his amateur contests after he had won the Commonwealth Games bantamweight gold medal at the age of 17. He then confessed to his trainer that he was doing 40 rounds of boxing in his home, purpose-built gym before his supervised training sessions! Barry was leaving all his strength and stamina in the gym, and he admits that it was not until he cut his training output by more than half that he started to show his full power and potential where and when it mattered – in the ring.

Pro-tip: Don't use your sparring sessions to try to become the king of the gymnasium. I have seen the confidence of boxers wrecked by stupidly going into every sparring bout with the objective of proving themselves the top dog in the gym. They always meet their master who puts them in their place when they try to take liberties. Your sparring bouts are the most important part of your gymnasium work and you must use them for the sole purpose of working on and improving specific combinations, counters and defensive moves. The gymnasium ring is a platform for skill not a punishment pit. Save your explosive energy for fight night.

8

Fight Day

Fight days become the longest days in the lives of boxers. If you are an amateur with school or work as a distraction the day might not drag quite as long as for a full-time professional with only the fight on his mind. My advice is that you relax as much as you possibly can. The only exercise I used to do on fight days was a brisk two-mile walk after a breakfast of grapefruit, a boiled or poached egg, a couple of slices of toast and marmalade and two cups of lemon tea or coffee. Never any fatty or fried food. After the walk I would play ten-card rummy with my twin brother, George, and then relax on my bed for a couple of hours before going off to the weigh-in.

I used to try to exude quiet confidence at the weigh-in and at the medical check. I was never a chat merchant like Muhammad Ali who would turn a weigh-in into a great theatrical event, but while I didn't do a lot of talking I thought it was important to let my opponent know that I was feeling in good nick. You can win psychological points by adopting an air of confidence at the weigh-in, although I wouldn't recommend anybody to go to Ali lengths because I am sure most boxers would find those acts he used to put on almost as exhausting as the fighting. Mind you, I recall that Ali brought out the showman in me at the weigh-in for our world title fight at Highbury Stadium in 1966. He was chipping and chatting on the scales and then we had to stand together for the photographers.

He was giving me the wide-eyed stare treatment and stealing all the publicity, but as I looked at him right up close I noticed one solitary black hair on his chest. I said loud enough for the posse of pressmen and the spectators to hear, 'Oh, look, he's a man all right, he's got a hair on his chest.' And I gave the hair a tweak. That brought the house down. They loved it. Ali didn't have his usual comeback and clammed right up after that. I had stolen his thunder and I had got myself a small but satisfying psychological victory. I'm not suggesting you go round pulling hair off the chests of your opponents, but don't be withdrawn and timid when coming face to face with them in pre-fight preliminaries.

After each weigh-in I used to go to a restaurant for my main meal of the day, a nice big rare steak with mixed salad. Avoid cucumber and onions and anything that can repeat on you. I would go for a stroll after lunch and then relax in bed for two or three hours. By then, of course, the fight was uppermost in my mind and I would mentally run over my tactical plans. Above all at this stage of proceedings you must avoid any negative thoughts. If you start thinking 'Suppose he knocks me out?' then you are asking for the thing you most fear. Be positive and have a mental picture of how you are going to win the fight.

After a light tea – avoid anything heavy for at least four hours before a contest – I liked to relax again for an hour. Then I left for the stadium, first of all checking that I had got everything in my boxing holdall. Gumshield, shorts, boxing boots, socks, protector, bandage and tape, ointments, soap and towels, dressing-gown, water bottle and a soft drink for after the fight.

I used to like to get to the arena about two hours before my contest. Some boxers prefer to leave it until the last possible moment before they arrive in the dressing-room, almost as if they are putting off the dreaded moment.

For me, the atmosphere of a dressing-room was just what I needed to get the adrenalin flowing and put me in the mood for the contest. I would have my hands bandaged at a leisurely pace, making sure they felt comfortable inside the protective bandage and tape. I liked a relaxed mood in the dressing-room but not to the point where your concentration wandered from the fight. The occasional wisecrack is okay, but you are there for serious business and laughter has to take a back seat. Even chatterboxer Muhammad Ali used to withdraw into himself once he was into the privacy of his dressing-room. For that last hour or so you should give the contest your total concentration.

About 30 minutes before you are due in the ring start warming-up, first of all with loosening jigging about exercises and then two or three rounds of fast shadow boxing. You should work up a light sweat before wrapping up ready for the walk to the ring.

Once into your corner keep moving lightly on your toes and practise a few side-steps so that you get used to the feel of the canvas. If it is slippery get some resin on the soles of your boots. Move to each side of the ring and test the tension of the ropes on your back.

When you are called to the centre of the ring for the final instructions from the referee look your opponent straight in the eye. Even if underneath you are as jumpy as a scared rabbit convince him you are brimming with confidence and self-belief.

The way I've described Fight Day is, of course, the way it was for me as a professional. But the message for any amateur is the same. Relax as much as possible ... eat sensibly and in good time to make sure you box on an empty stomach ... make sure your hands are bandaged properly ... warm-up in the dressing-room ... don't let your opponent think you are anything less than 100 per cent confident in the pre-fight preliminaries.

My final words to you as the 'seconds out' call comes before the first bell would be: 'Hands up ... keep cool ... good luck!'

9
It's a Knock-out

It's every boxer's dream to land the perfect knock-out blow. There is nothing more satisfying than to fire home a punch or a combination and see your opponent going down and out for the count. Everybody wants to be a knock-out specialist but it is a gift given to few boxers and it is something you cannot teach. In my experience, knock-out punchers are not manufactured but are blessed with a natural knack of timing and delivering their punches.

You can develop and improve your punching power, but that real knock-out weapon has to be with you from the start. It just doesn't happen that boxers suddenly, overnight, turn into punchers. A punch has little to do with muscles or strength; it's all a matter of reflexes and timing. The legendary Jimmy Wilde, world flyweight champion before the First World War, never weighed more than seven and a half stone wet through and was as thin as a matchstick, yet he could knock out welterweights. In boxing a punching muscle is long and sinewy, not a bunched muscle such as a weight-lifter or body-builder gets.

Most of the great punchers have had the knack of meeting a man as he's coming onto the punch, which doubles its effectiveness with the weight of both boxers then being involved. It's like a head-on collision between two cars as opposed to the kind of crash where a car hits something that gives.

In my own experience, the best knock-out punches travel no further than about nine inches. There have of course been plenty of champions specializing in long-range knock-out blows (Rocky Marciano, Ingemar Johansson, Jack Dempsey, Sonny Liston, Mike Tyson and Tommy Hearns spring to mind). But the outstanding knock-out specialists – the likes of Joe Louis, Archie Moore, Sugar Ray Robinson, Roberto Duran and Colin Jones – devastated their opponents with short, sharp punches.

Turn the shoulder. *There have been few punchers in history to match the knockout power of Joe Louis at his peak. Here he lifts challenger Tami Mauriello off his feet with a half hook, half cross that finished the world title fight after just two minutes nine seconds of the first round. Just look at the way Louis has generated the power from his shoulder. His shoulders have swung almost as much as if he had an invisible golf club in his hands. He is set up to finish Mauriello off with a right cross as he swings his shoulders back in the opposite direction*

I was one of the lucky ones blessed with natural knock-out power. At the peak of my career some research work was done on the speed and strength of my left hook by a scientific team from the RAF's Institute of Aviation Medicine headed by Flight

Lieutenant Dick Borland, a bio-physicist who analysed 6,600 pictures of my punch that were taken by a special high-speed camera in just six seconds. My left fist's acceleration over five and a half inches was found to equal 60 times the force of gravity. At the end of the five and a half inches the fist was travelling at 30 m.p.h. with the whole body weight behind it. The punch, Dick Borland said, lasted only 48 thousandths of a second and even when they slowed it down more than 40 times it was still too fast for the eye to see. They projected 80 frames, one by one, and they were able to measure the distance the fist travelled every five frames.

This scientific analysis revealed that when I started to launch the left hook it travelled 15 times faster than the Saturn Five rocket that takes astronauts to the moon. The force on landing approached three tons. I relate these facts just to underline that a knock-out punch flows naturally because I could not possibly have been taught how to generate such power.

As far as I was concerned I used to throw my favourite left hook as much by instinct as anything. I didn't stop to think about it. It would be impossible for me to explain how to throw a punch with the sort of force I used to be able to muster. Obviously I developed and improved the punch over the years but the raw power was there to begin with and came to me quite naturally. It amuses me when I see instruction books including chapters on how to become a knock-out puncher. If it could be taught, the boxing world would be full of knock-out specialists. All I can do is stress that you must continually practise until your punches become smooth and spontaneous. It is not necessarily the hardest punches that bring a knock-out victory but the best timed. George Foreman hit Muhammad Ali with a procession of heavy punches during their world title fight in Zaire in 1974. But the punch that finished the fight – a straight right counter to the jaw as Ali came off the ropes – had much less raw power than Foreman's punches. It was just that Ali's timing was perfect.

Just about the best knock-out punch I ever landed was against Welsh giant Dick Richardson at Porthcawl in 1958. A rough, tough fighter, Richardson had cut my eye with a butt in the first round and in the fifth he knocked me down with a swinging right to the head.

I deliberately pretended that I was hurt more badly than I

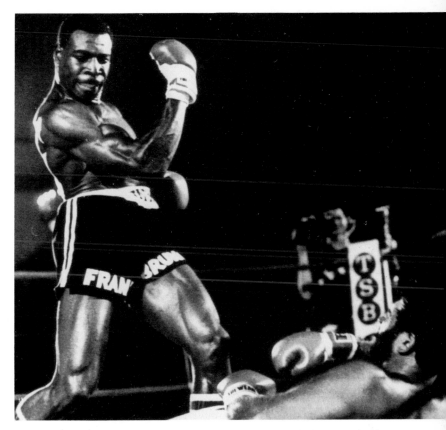

The follow-through. *This is the finish of the best combination of punches that Frank Bruno threw on his way to championship contention. A left hook scattered the senses of Mike Jameson and Bruno followed up with a huge right uppercut that sent the American crashing backwards to be counted out in their fight in Chicago in July 1983. My reason for including the picture in this instruction book is Frank's follow-through. He has kept the punch going long after connection. I make no excuse for continually referring to the follow-through aspect of punching. In my experience, not enough trainers and coaches make sufficient noise to their boxers about it. If you go to a golf professional for a lesson he will keep on repeating: 'Hit through the ball.' Well, I will keep on repeating: 'Punch through the target'*

actually was, and when I got up at a count of eight Dick came charging at me like a wild bull with his guard down. I met him with a left hook bang on the point of the jaw. It took him off his feet about six inches and he crashed backwards, out to the world. The referee didn't complete the formality of the count but as far as I was concerned that was as satisfying a knock-out punch as I had ever thrown.

Richardson, who later won the European heavyweight championship, took my punch on the point of the chin, the most vulnerable spot for potential knock-out blows. Other sensitive areas are the temples, the edges of the jawbone beneath the ear, the nerve centre directly beneath the nose, the solar plexus, the liver, just beneath or over the heart, and below the ribs to the front and side of the body.

Lloyd Honeyghan revealed how effective a punch to the solar plexus can be when he knocked out Mexican Jorge Vaca at Wembley in March 1988 to regain the world welterweight title. His right hand sunk deep into Vaca's body and knocked all the breath and the fight out of him.

It was a perfect delivery of a solar plexus punch, and Lloyd cleared the way for it with a two-fisted attack to the head that forced Vaca to raise his guard and leave his body unprotected.

When attempting to deliver a knock-out blow you must have your front foot planted firmly on the canvas and get your body-weight behind the punch. The most important thing of all is to follow through with the punch. Only the cleverest counter-punchers can land knock-out blows while their weight is on the back foot, when most of the power comes from the fact that the boxer on the receiving end is moving forward at the moment of impact.

10

The Cooper Commandments

Ten golden rules that you should adopt if you are going to box the champions' way:

1 Never get into the ring less than 100 per cent fit. Physical fitness is all important.

2 Find a trainer whom you respect and then listen to him.

3 Cultivate a strong jab. It's the foundation punch for all boxers.

4 Punch through the target, not at it.

5 Don't be predictable and stereotyped. Box with imagination and invention.

6 Get the miles in on the road. Strong legs help maketh a strong boxer.

7 Find out as much as you possibly can about your opponent's strengths and weaknesses.

8 Don't be a stationary target and never move around the ring on a predictable path.

9 Relax as much as possible on fight day but have a good warm-up session in the dressing-room before going into the ring.

10 Defend yourself at all times.

11
The Final Round

As the final round in this guide to boxing the champions' way, here is a mixed bag of refresher tips that could help you whether you are a beginner or an accomplished fighter. I shall be repeating several of the points I have made in the previous sections because I feel you cannot stress them too often:

Try not to be a predictable, stereotyped opponent. The more variety and invention you can bring to your ring work the harder you will be to beat. Do not, for instance, lean too heavily on the same feinting trick because your opponent will fathom it out and will be ready to launch a counter-attack while you are briefly unguarded. And don't be predictable with your punch pattern. Remember you can use hooks, swings and uppercuts as well as the basic straight punches. Double up on your punches, particularly the jab. Punch with the knuckle part of the closed glove.

Practise hooking off the jab. The beauty of the hook following the straight jab is that it comes out of your opponent's line of vision and can be a great surprise to him. Twist your wrist just

---

The unexpected. It sometimes pays to manufacture punches that are not in the boxing manuals. Here's one that I created on the spur of the moment to surprise my old foe Joe Erskine. He was anticipating a body attack and my improvised right to the nose came as quite a shock. Try not to be too predictable and orthodox. You can often swing a close contest your way by suddenly doing something completely unpredictable

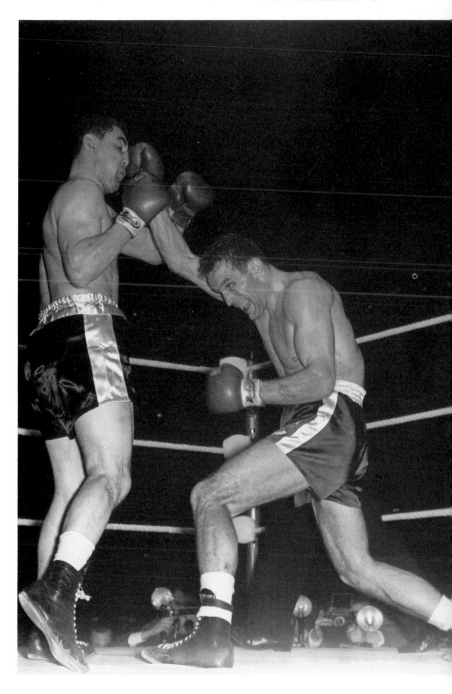

before the moment of impact and screw the hook punch into the target.

When delivering your hardest punches take half a step forward making sure your front foot is in line with your opponent, otherwise your punches could fall short of their target. Get your shoulder behind the punch.

If you are a superior boxer matched with a heavier hitting opponent, make up your mind to dictate the contest with skill. No matter what, don't let him lure you into a fight. Box. Don't fight.

Don't throw 'arm' punches unless it's for range-finding or to deceive your opponent into thinking you are a 'tap' puncher. Your punches should come from the shoulder with your body-weight behind them. Punch *through* the target not *at* it. In short, punch your weight.

Don't advertise your punches. If you telegraph what you are about to do with exaggerated movements you will give your opponent time to take evasive action and prepare a counter-attack. The moment you have landed your punches get your hands back into defensive positions to protect your head and body.

Boxing is the art of deception. Practise body feints and throwing 'phantom' punches in the gymnasium until you have a complete bag of tricks with which to confuse and bemuse your opponent. Don't become a one-trick artist. You will quickly get found out.

If you are up against a specialist left hooker, circle to your left and keep your right hand guarding your chin and your elbow tucked into your side.

If you are up against a specialist right-hand hitter, circle to your right and keep your left hand guarding your chin and your elbow tucked into your side.

If you are up against a powerful two-handed puncher, keep your chin tucked behind your left shoulder and keep changing direction. Remember it's harder to hit a moving target.

If you are matched with a shorter opponent, fire as many straight punches as possible because this will allow you to make the most of your height and reach advantage.

If fighting a taller opponent look for every opportunity to step inside and counter to the head and body; use the ring to cut his angles and trap him in corners.

If you are up against a southpaw, circle in a clockwise direction away from his left hand and keep your left hand high to guard against right hooks. Try to lure him into your left hook, thrown over his right jab. Look for the chance to parry his right lead and counter with a straight right to the chin. When slipping his lead be prepared to block his left with your right hand.

Try not to be lured into leading against a renowned counter-puncher. Use your feints to try to draw him forward. Counter as quickly as possible yourself once you have avoided his counters.

Employ the right uppercut against a shorter opponent who comes rushing in with head-down, bulldozing tactics. You can also keep him off balance with quick side-steps. Don't let him drive you onto the ropes. Back him up as often as possible and try to be first to the punch.

If you are tired, hurt by a punch or worried about an injury, do your best not to show it. Become a poker-face in the ring. Don't let facial expressions give your opponent confidence and hope.

Always warm up in the dressing-room before a contest with several rounds of shadow boxing. Work up a light sweat and then make sure you are warmly wrapped up before going to the ring.

You can gain important psychological advantages even before a punch is thrown. Give the impression of quiet confidence at the weigh-in, and during the pre-fight instructions in the ring look your opponent straight in the eye. Even the greatest champions experience big-fight nerves. Just don't let it show to your opponent.

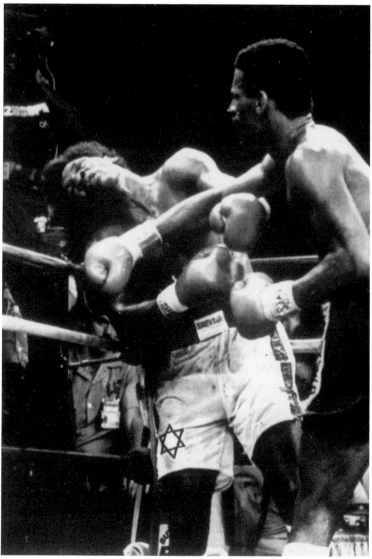

Trapped in the corner. *John Davis learns the hard way that you must never get trapped in the corner in boxing. He had nowhere to hide as Mike Spinks unleashed this crushing right cross punch that forced the referee's intervention in the ninth round of their world light-heavyweight championship fight in Atlantic City in 1982. If you get cornered, keep your hands high and your elbows together*

Make full use of the precious minute you have between each round. Listen to what you are being told and follow your instructions. Your second will be able to see things from his wide angle that can escape your attention from close range. Ask your second to keep his instructions brief and to the point. A long-winded cornerman can confuse a boxer if he tries to stress too many points. Also insist that only one person does the talking in the corner. You can become bewildered by having two or more seconds talking across each other and offering differing advice.

When sitting in the corner between rounds make sure both feet are on the ground, keep your arms down and your hands resting on your knees. Take deep breaths and keep your arms and legs as relaxed as possible. Don't slouch on your stool.

Don't unload all your best punches and moves in the first round. Keep as much hidden from your opponent as possible until you have weighed up his strengths and weaknesses.

When working at close quarters, try to get your arms inside your opponent's. Stand square-on and keep your weight balanced evenly. Get your head lower than your opponent's and keep your elbows tucked into your sides. Twist your trunk when delivering your punches to increase the power. Switch the direction of your attack from the body to the head and then back again. If you must hold, do it on the referee's blindside. Have both your hands up for protection when breaking from a clinch.

One of the first essentials of a successful boxer is quick and clever footwork. Practise keeping on your toes and moving both ways as smoothly and smartly as possible. You should have both feet planted on the canvas only when throwing your hardest punches or when at close quarters. Don't stand with your feet too wide apart because this will restrict your mobility, and be careful not to let your feet cross. Work at improving your rhythm and agility by quick and varied rope skipping.

Take every opportunity to knock your opponent off balance. This can be achieved by a simple nudge of his shoulder as he is

Tricks of the trade. *Muhammad Ali knew – and used – every trick in the book during his illustrious career. Here we see him defusing Sonny Liston's dynamite by the simple tactic of forcing his head down with the palm of his glove. The effect was to make Sonny lose his balance and distance. Ali – or Cassius Clay as he was then – won this February 1964 title fight to become new world heavyweight champion when Liston retired with a mystery shoulder injury at the end of the sixth round*

about to deliver a punch. You can also put him off balance by wrong-footing him with intelligent side-stepping.

Conserve your energy if you are in a long-distance fight but without surrendering the initiative. Take advantage of stamina-saving clinches, making sure you rest your weight on your opponent, not vice versa. There's also the skill of manoeuvring your opponent so that you finish each round as close as possible to your own corner when the bell rings. Listen for 'last ten' shouts from your second which will be the signal that there are just ten seconds to the bell and time to be getting close to your corner. It also saves your legs if you can 'boss' the centre of the ring, making your opponent use precious energy circling around you.

If you must take breathers on the ropes make sure you protect yourself properly behind cover guards and roll with the punches to minimize their power. Don't get yourself trapped in a corner. If you do, make sure you adopt the full or cross cover method of defence with your arms knife-jacked protecting your body and with your gloves high in front of your face.

If you are knocked down, don't jump straight up. Get on one knee as quickly as possible and try to look to your corner for signals. Have a plan in mind for when you rise to your feet; this could involve the delivery of a punch aimed at catching your opponent as he comes forward, clinching and smothering tactics or you can 'get on your bike' and circle away from his most powerful punches. The vital thing when you get up is that you should have your hands held high and your elbows tucked into your sides.

If you are unlucky enough to get a cut eye during a contest, make sure you get your nearest hand up high to guard it. Circle away and keep your opponent at a distance until you can get back to your corner for treatment. Keep out of clinches and avoid having the eye rubbed.

Never lose your temper in the ring. Always maintain your self-control and keep trying to out-think your opponent. Stay cool and calm in any crisis. Don't be impetuous and remember that in the boxing ring patience is a virtue.

Be respectful of the referee and listen to his instructions.

Use gymnasium sparring sessions to improve your technique and skills, *not* to prove yourself king of the gym. Work out with sparring partners of all shapes, sizes and styles. Always wear a headguard, big gloves and a gumshield. Never be a bully in the gym by taking advantage of a weaker, less skilful sparring partner. It will not only make you unpopular, but somebody superior to you will eventually give you the same treatment.

Be careful not to overtrain. Work out with weights only under supervision.

Put your miles in on the road to strengthen your legs and stamina. Try not to run where traffic exhaust and fumes are polluting the air.

If you are an amateur, join an ABA-affiliated club and listen carefully to the trainers. Be sure to practise all the skill techniques and accept that you can always get better. Try to look smart in the ring. The boxer who takes pride in his appearance also takes pride in his performance.

Above all remember that the Noble Art of boxing is to hit your opponent without being hit yourself. Ignore the defensive skills at your peril. Don't forget boxing's oldest saying: you must defend yourself at all times.

My final advice is that you should take every opportunity to watch the great champions in action, whether in the flesh or on film. There is something you can learn from every one of them. To become a champion at boxing you have to box the champions' way.